Contents

War Begins

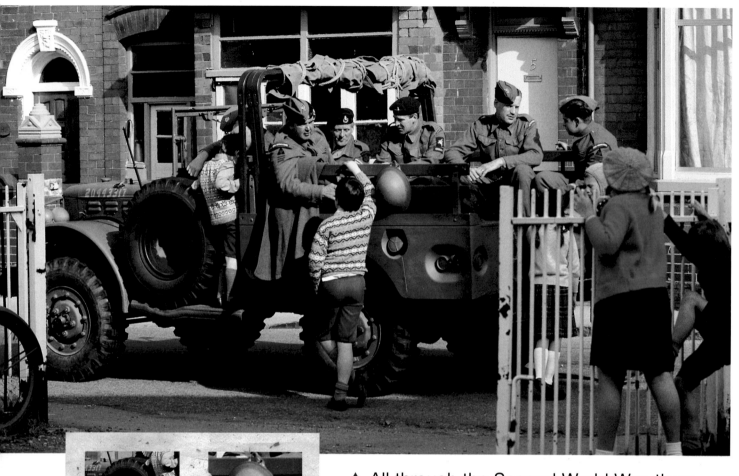

spare wheel

hard hat

soft roof

jeep

▲ All through the Second World War, there were soldiers on the streets.

In 1933, Adolf Hitler became the leader of Germany. Hitler wanted Germany to have more land and power in Europe.

In 1938, Germany invaded Austria and Czechoslovakia. Then, on 1 September 1939, Germany invaded Poland. The leaders of France and Britain had promised to help Poland if Hitler invaded. On 3 September, Britain declared war against Germany. It was the start of the Second World War.

filter

plastic window

instructions

▲ A gas mask felt tight and made it hard to breathe.

The British government knew that German planes would probably bomb British cities. The country had to prepare for air raids.

The government was afraid that Hitler's air force would drop bombs with poisonous gas on Britain. In 1938, it gave everyone a gas mask. People had to carry one in case there was a gas attack. There were different masks for adults, children, babies and even animals!

In the first few weeks of war, schools and workplaces had gas-mask drills. People learnt what to do if there was a gas attack. Children hated putting on their gas masks. They smelt of rubber and made them feel sick.

Evacuation

▲ People left the cities by train.

gas mask box

suitcases

label

trolley

guard

The British government was afraid that people in cities would be hurt by the bombings. It evacuated mothers and children to the countryside.

Evacuation began on 1 September 1939. The evacuees went to stay with families in safe areas of the countryside.

About 1.5 million children between the ages of 5 and 14 years old were evacuated. Mothers of children under 5 were evacuated, too. The children took a few clothes and a gas mask. They wore a label showing their name and address.

The children travelled to the countryside on the train. When they arrived, they met their host family. It was hard living with strangers. Some children and host families got on well. Others didn't like each other at all!

By January 1940 there had been no air raids. More than half of the evacuees returned home to the cities. Yet the air raids were still to come.

▲ These posters gave people advice about evacuation, gas masks and transport.

Rationing

In 1939 Germany started to attack the ships that brought food to Britain. On 8 January 1940, the government brought in rationing. This made sure people had enough to eat.

▼ This is a grocer's shop during the war.

| none left! | first-aid kit | scales | sweets | custard | stock cubes |

▲ This was one person's food ration for a week in September 1940.

Everyone had a ration book with coupons for different foods. Butter, sugar, meat, tea and other foods were rationed.

In spring 1941, new types of food appeared in the shops. They replaced fresh foods that people could not buy. There were powdered eggs, tinned milk, and tinned meat called Spam.

Not all foods were rationed. For example, people could always buy bread and they could buy sauces to make their food taste better.

The rations look very small to us today. Yet rationing made sure that British people did not starve during the war.

4oz (100g) butter

2oz (50g) tea

4oz (100g) bacon

1 egg

1oz (25g) cheese

8oz (200g) sugar

ration book

Wartime Clothes

▲ This shop shows prices in coupons.

dress

broken window   price list

The government needed Britain's factories to make goods for the war. Making clothes was less important. In 1941, the government brought in clothes rationing.

Every person had a clothing ration book. It contained enough coupons to buy one outfit with underwear, and nightclothes. It had to last 15 months.

The government told people to make their clothes last longer. They had to 'make do and mend'. Women mended old clothes. They made children's clothes out of curtains and coats out of old blankets.

Stockings were very hard to find. Instead, many women covered their legs with gravy browning (which was used to make gravy go browner). They drew a line down the back of their legs to look like a seam. It was hard to find make-up, too. Women used beetroot juice as lipstick.

Clothes in the war were very plain. They were made with as little material as possible. Skirts were knee length. Trousers had no turn-ups. Hats were not rationed though, so women wore the most glamorous hats they could find.

▼ Here you can see ration books, money and an identity card.

identity card

child's ration book

stamp

clothing ration book

bus tickets

food ration book

11

Dig for Victory!

Before the war, Britain bought lots of fruit and vegetables from other countries. When the war began, people had to grow their own. They grew vegetables that grew quickly, such as potatoes, carrots, onions, cabbages and peas.

▼ A father and his children grow vegetables on their allotment.

| hoe | onions | potatoes | cabbages | bucket |

In October 1939, the government asked people to 'Dig for Victory'. It wanted everyone to grow vegetables to help the war effort. People learned how to grow vegetables on allotments. Women and children worked on the allotments because many men were away fighting the war.

People found all kinds of places to grow food. They put soil on the roofs of air-raid shelters. They planted beans and beetroot on football pitches and near railways. Even the gardens at Buckingham Palace became allotments.

Government posters told people to eat vegetables for their vitamins. The British people needed to be healthy to win the war.

▲ These government posters showed people on the home front how they could help their country.

Food

Women had to think of clever ways of using the food rations to feed their families. In the mornings, they listened to advice on a radio programme called *The Kitchen Front*.

Sugar was rationed, so cooks learnt to use beetroots, carrots and parsnips to make puddings. They made pastry from potatoes to save butter.

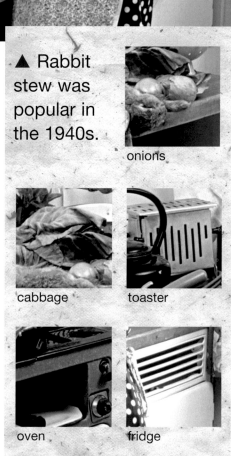

▲ Rabbit stew was popular in the 1940s.

onions

cabbage

toaster

oven

fridge

▲ These were some of the foods people ate during the war.

Meat was important for protein. Some people kept chickens, rabbits or pigs in their garden. Others joined a 'pig club'. They gave their food scraps to a farmer, to feed a pig. When the pig was killed, they shared the meat.

People were careful not to waste food. They cooked every part of the pig. They even cooked the trotters (feet) and the tail.

Most people ate better during the war than before. They ate more fruit and vegetables, and less fat and sugar. Wartime meals were healthier than some of the food we eat today!

cabbage

dripping

liver, kidney

tripe, onions

dried egg recipe

pig's trotter and tail

Free Time

There was no TV during the Second World War. In their free time, people sewed, knitted, read, or did jigsaw puzzles.

In the evening, everyone closed their black-out curtains. They made sure no light showed through the windows. Lights could show German pilots where to drop their bombs.

People mostly stayed at home in the evening. The black-out made it too dark to go out. They listened to news of the war on the radio.

▼ A quiet evening at home.

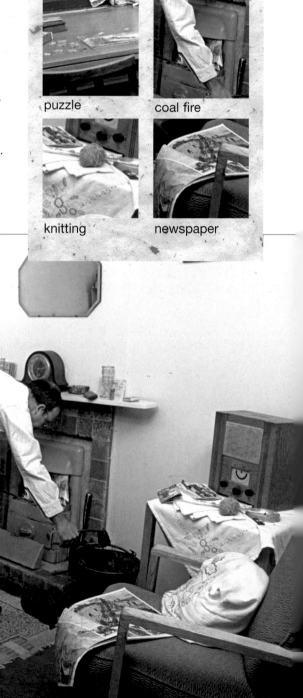

radio

sewing machine

puzzle

coal fire

knitting

newspaper

needle

tuning knobs

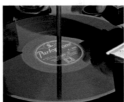
record

▲ This is a radiogram – a combined radio and a record player.

Many people enjoyed hearing Britain's prime minister, Winston Churchill, on the radio. He told them to keep working hard to win the war.

To cheer everyone up, there were songs by Vera Lynn, dance music and comedy shows. Children listened to 'Larry the Lamb' on *Children's Hour*.

Sometimes, people went to the cinema. They watched films like *Gone with the Wind*.

Women's Work

Early in the war, 43,000 women volunteered to join the women's services. They joined the women's branch of the army, the air force or the navy.

At first, most women did office work or cooking. Later, their work became more exciting. In the women's air force, they flew planes to air bases, and worked as mechanics. In the army, women aimed guns at enemy aircraft. They were not allowed to shoot though!

▲ A member of the women's army.

▲ The mangle squeezed water out of wet clothes.

mangle   wash boiler   iron   pegs

Women had important jobs at home, too. They worked hard to save fuel. When they did the laundry, they used as little coal and electricity as possible.

Women also looked after evacuees, and children whose mothers were working in the factories.

Some women joined the Women's Voluntary Service (WVS). They made food for rescue workers and people whose homes had been bombed.

Children

Children helped to win the war, too. They collected materials for recycling.

The British government wanted people to collect metal, glass, clothes and paper. In 1940, the government asked for aluminium to help make fighter planes.

jars   wheelbarrow

clothes   pan

Women gave away pots and pans. Children gave up their metal toys and bikes. Most of the items were recycled.

▲ Children collected goods for recycling in wheelbarrows.

Children still had time to play. They loved looking for bits of metal from fallen German planes. It was dangerous to play in some streets though. Houses that had been damaged by bombs sometimes fell down.

At home, children read comics like *The Beano* and *The Dandy*. They played games about war, such as Air Sea Rescue. A popular game was darts – with Hitler as the bulls-eye!

During the war, children missed out on Guy Fawkes' night. It was banned because of the rules of the black-out.

▲ Children played with things they found outdoors.

Air Raid!

The first German air raid was on London, on 7 September 1940. Soon other big cities were hit, too. During air raids, people were supposed to go to shelters.

▶ A brick air-raid shelter.

▼ A Morrison shelter in a living room.

wire side

steel table top

At the beginning of the war, the government built brick air-raid shelters and gave people Anderson shelters to put in their gardens. Yet many people decided to stay in their homes.

In 1941 the government brought in Morrison shelters. These were large, steel tables to use inside homes. People could shelter under them during an air raid.

The Blitz

▲ An air-raid warden looks for survivors.

From September 1940 to May 1941, German bomber planes attacked Britain at night. This was called 'the Blitz'.

The bombs hit cities, ports and factories. In London, the Blitz went on for 57 nights in a row. Thousands of people were killed. Many homes, shops and factories were ruined. In November 1940, German bombs destroyed the city of Coventry.

After an air raid, fire fighters, ambulance workers and air-raid wardens rushed to rescue people.

air-raid warden

torch

bomb

Some bombs did not go off straight away. They were called unexploded bombs (UXBs). People who lived near a UXB had to move away until it had been made safe.

The V1 and V2 bombs were even more frightening. They were so quiet that people did not hear them until they exploded. In London, they killed over 8,000 people and injured 22,000. Hitler used V1s and V2s from 1944–45. Yet by this time, Germany was losing the war.

sandbags

KEEP CLEAR
UNEXPLODED
BOMB

danger sign

air-raid warden

▼ An air-raid warden warns a boy about a UXB.

KEEP CLEAR
UNEXPLODED
BOMB

A New Britain

On 8 May 1945, Britain celebrated Victory in Europe (VE) Day. The war in Europe had ended at last.

People looked forward to better times. First, the government had to build new houses. Nearly 500,000 homes had been destroyed in the war. New houses were also needed for the 2 million people who had got married during the war. By January 1948, the government had built nearly 160,000 prefabricated homes, or 'prefabs'.

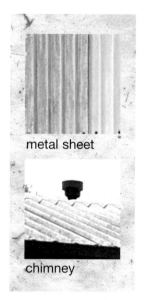

metal sheet

chimney

▼ The prefabs were made from recycled metal.

For many people, the prefabs were better than their home before the war. For the first time, they had a bathroom with hot running water and an indoor toilet. They had a gas fridge and an electric stove. A coal fire in the living room kept the house warm and heated the water.

All prefabs had a garden. They were usually built in groups, so people had neighbours. Most people were very happy with their new home. Many prefabs were still in use over 40 years later.

running water

shaving soap

▼ The bathroom in a prefab house.

Timeline

1939

April
All men aged 20 and 21 can be called up to join the British armed forces.

1 September
Germany invades Poland.

In Britain, the black-out is brought in.

Evacuation begins.

3 September
Britain, France, Australia and New Zealand declare war on Germany.

Men between 18 and 41 can be called up to join the British army, navy or air force.

October
The government asks people to 'Dig for Victory'.

1940

8 January
Food rationing is brought in for the first time.

9 April
Germany invades Norway and Denmark.

10 May
Germany invades the Netherlands, Luxembourg, Belgium and France.

Winston Churchill becomes prime minister.

10 July
The Battle of Britain begins.

September
The Battle of Britain ends. Germany begins to bomb British cities.

7 September
The London Blitz begins.

14 November
Coventry is destroyed by bombing.

1941

6 April
Germany invades Yugoslavia and Greece.

May
The Blitz ends.

1 June
Clothes rationing is brought in.

22 June
Germany invades the USSR (the Union of Soviet Socialist Republics, which included Russia and other nearby countries).

11 December
Germany and Italy declare war on the USA.

1942

February
Soap is rationed.

April
Germany starts bombing Exeter, Norwich, York, Canterbury and Bath.

1943

31 January
The Germans surrender in the USSR.

3 May
Women between 18 and 45 have to do war work.

1944

6 June
D-Day landings in France.

1945

8 May
Germany is defeated. Victory in Europe Day is declared.

Glossary

air base A place where military aircraft fly from.

air raid When aircraft drop bombs on an area.

air-raid shelter A shelter to protect people from bomb attacks. Some were buried in the ground. Others were indoors.

air-raid warden Person who helped to keep people safe during an air raid.

allotment A piece of land for growing vegetables.

Anderson shelter An air-raid shelter dug under the ground in a garden.

black-out At night, all the time it was dark, when any lights had to be covered so they could not be seen.

Blitz, the The German air raids against Britain from 1940–41.

coupon A piece of paper that people gave to a shopkeeper in return for their rations.

drill A way of remembering something by practising it many times.

dripping Fat collected from boiled or roasted beef.

evacuation The movement of people to a safer place.

evacuee Person who has been moved to a safer place.

gas mask A mask that protects against breathing poisonous gas.

gravy browning Powder that made gravy look dark brown.

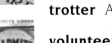

host family A family that had evacuees staying in their home.

identity card A card showing a person's name and address.

invade To enter a country with an army to take it over.

mechanic A person who repairs machines.

Morrison shelter A steel table that protected people during an air raid.

prefabricated home (prefab) A building made in sections that can be put together.

protein A substance found in meat, eggs, fish and some vegetables that helps people to grow and stay healthy.

rationing Rules that allow people to have a fixed amount of food, fuel or other goods.

siren A machine that makes a loud sound to warn people.

Spam A kind of tinned meat, made mainly from ham.

tripe The stomach lining of a cow or pig, eaten as food.

trotter A pig's foot.

volunteered Offered to work without being paid.

wash boiler An early form of washing machine.

women's services Branches of the army or navy that were for women only.

Activities

pp4–5 War Begins

- In a history atlas or on the Internet, find a map showing Europe at the start of the Second World War. Trace the map and mark on it the countries that Hitler invaded in 1938 and 1939.

- When you next visit a museum, look out for old gas masks. Design a poster with instructions for what to do in a gas attack.

- Find out about the different kinds of gas masks, and how gas masks were used on babies.

pp6–7 Evacuation

- Read the book *Carrie's War* by Nina Bawden, or watch the film.

- Imagine what it was like to be an evacuee. What would you pack in your suitcase? Write a letter home to your parents telling them about life in your new home.

pp8–9 Rationing

- Look in library books or on the Internet for some wartime recipes.

- Plan your own meal using rationed foods and fresh vegetables.

- Weigh some wartime food rations.

pp10–11 Wartime Clothes

- Find out about clothes in the Second World War from library books or the Internet. Compare the fashions then with today's fashions.

pp12–13 Dig for Victory!

- Find out which vegetables grow well in your area. Check when the seeds should be planted.

- Draw a plan of a vegetable patch, showing the position of the vegetables.

- Design your own poster for the 'Dig for Victory' campaign.

pp14–15 Food

- Use the food on page 15 to write a menu for a dinner party during the Second World War.

- Ask people who lived through the war about the food they ate in wartime.

- Draw a plan showing how you could keep rabbits, pigs and chickens in a playing field or garden.

pp16–17 Free Time

- Talk to a friend or family member who lived through the war. Find out how they spent their free time.

- Look at the picture on page 16. Imagine you are at home during the Second World War. Write a diary describing your day.

pp18–19 Women's Work

- Make a list of all the items in the kitchen on page 19. Compare them to the machines in your kitchen.

- Find out about the different kinds of jobs that women did during the war.

pp20–21 Children

- Go round your school collecting goods for recycling, like children did during the war. Sort out the materials and think about how each one could be reused or recycled.

pp22–23 Air Raid!

- Write simple instructions for what to do in an air raid.

- Find out if there are any old air-raid shelters near where you live. Some people have an Anderson shelter in their garden.

- Write a list of things you would need in an air-raid shelter.

pp24–25 The Blitz

- Go to your local library or museum and find out if your local area was bombed during the war. Visit the places that were bombed and look at the buildings. Which buildings do you think survived the war and which were built after the war?

- Imagine your home is destroyed by a bomb. Write some adjectives to describe how you might feel.

pp26–27 A New Britain

- Visit your local Record Office. Look at maps from 1945–50. Find out if any prefab houses were built. See if you can visit some prefab homes.

Find Out More

BOOKS TO READ

Growing up in World War II: Entertainment; Food; Getting About; School by C. Burch (Franklin Watts, 2009)

History Snapshots: Children and World War II by Sarah Ridley (Franklin Watts, 2011)

Horrible History: The Blitzed Brits by Terry Deary (Scholastic, 2007)

In the War: The Blitz by Simon Adams (Wayland, 2008)

In the War: Food; School Life by Peter Hicks (Wayland, 2008)

The Story of a World War II Evacuee by Andrew Donkin (Wayland, 2008)

PLACES TO VISIT

Avoncroft Museum of Historic Buildings, Worcestershire
www.avoncroft.org.uk/
Important buildings from the past, including prefab houses.

Flambards Village Theme Park, Cornwall
www.flambards.co.uk/
At this theme park, you can see what life was like during the Blitz.

The Imperial War Museum London, Duxford (Cambridgeshire) and North (Manchester)
www.iwm.org.uk/
Everything to do with the Second World War, including the Home Front.

Index

Page numbers in **bold** mean there is a photo on the page.